The Americanized Gospel

The Americanized Gospel

Can the American Catholic Church Remain
Authentic under Nationalism?

JOHN M. JERPE

RESOURCE *Publications* · Eugene, Oregon

THE AMERICANIZED GOSPEL
Can the American Catholic Church Remain Authentic under Nationalism?

Resource Publications
An Imprint of Wipf and Stock Publishers
199 W. 8th Ave., Suite 3
Eugene, OR 97401

www.wipfandstock.com

PAPERBACK ISBN: 979-8-3852-1303-0
HARDCOVER ISBN: 979-8-3852-1304-7
EBOOK ISBN: 979-8-3852-1305-4

VERSION NUMBER 03/13/24

Contents

Preface
This Is a Simple Little Book

THIS SIMPLE LITTLE BOOK is written for the people who need it: not because they are simple or little but because they are hard-working, busy Catholic family people who are being left out of a very important conversation that this simple little book tries to address. They have shouldered all of the trials and responsibilities that come with raising Catholic families while trying to "make ends meet." But the point is that that "busy-ness" withholds that conversation from them. Although this book is about our Catholic Faith, it is also about something that threatens it.

I have read a number of books and articles about the issues that are included in this book, namely the issues of peace and justice, nationalism, the military industrial complex, and a few other issues and I have tried to connect those writings with our collective prayer life as a people.

I have noticed that typically, when a Catholic author addresses these issues (peace and justice, nationalism, the military industrial complex, etc.), they are, for the most part, written by Catholic theologians, philosophers, and people generally regarded as intellectuals. But the unfortunate fact is that the material written about these issues talked about herein by our Catholic theologians, philosophers, and intellectuals tend to be read by only by one another. They are rarely read by working people; the Catholic intelligentsia is "preaching to the choir."

Because we are so busy trying to "make ends meet" we are the people most easily victimized by the powers that distract and use us, and lure us into needless, even harmful loyalties, largely through empty promises of security and a perverted notion of freedom. The issues discussed herein and named above and the resulting spiritual concerns unquestionably require our attention.

Many Catholics will not want to hear this, and they may turn away from this conversation now, but I suspect that the "Americanized" Catholic Church, with an "Americanized" Gospel, is on a collision course with a falsity of our own making, the falsity of a people called to holiness but engulfed by the false promises of nationalism. God willing, as a people, with a little courage and humility, we will read, learn, and think more about the nature of that falsity. It is at the very least annoying, but we owe it to ourselves, our children, our grandchildren and to our parishes to consider changing our way of talking and thinking about these issues. These issues come with nationalism, and we are called to look more carefully at our faith.

I hope that together we can not only talk about these issues (peace and justice, nationalism, and also the military industrial complex) but also about our national lives as we address these issues. I hope to effectively urge that when it comes to the above issues, we as a people might be "in denial" or looking the other way.

I know that as Americans it is easier to live with an "Americanized Gospel" than it is to challenge our assumptions about the way we think about our world. Those of us who need to talk with one another about these issues the most are the salesmen, the parish bible study groups, and the retirees who volunteer at the parish kitchens. They are the workers from all of the trades and the areas in which people labor the hardest to "make ends meet," to send their children to decent schools, and to meet the ever-rising cost of health care for their families.

It is for that reason that this "simple little book" is suggested. We are not fools, but we are busy, even to a self-destructive extent. That is why we may feel so terribly threatened and unsettled and even annoyed when these issues are raised.

This simple book and the spiritual issues that flow from addressing these "issues" should not intimidate any of the good people for whom it is written, although it will necessarily annoy some of us. While Catholic journalists, theologians, philosophers, and intellectuals write about, say, the Just War Theory, (and hopefully about the modern-day consequences of its attempted application), I will hope that my involvement in the Peace and Justice movement over the years and the reading and studying I have done will effectively address some of the avoidable mistakes we are making. I have tried to remain reasonably informed about my faith as a practicing Catholic. Now we must look at ourselves in relation to the rest of the world.

But I also have a son and a daughter in their mid-fifties, both working people, and they each have two very young children. They and their Catholic families are or will become the type of people for whom this book is written. Lastly, I hope that whether or not I live to see it, my four grandchildren, as adults, will enjoy safe drinking water, breathe clean air, and enjoy a predictable world and a reliable food supply and that they are not enjoying them at the expense of anyone else.

1

The Just War Theory

THIS BOOK BEGINS WITH a brief discussion of the Just War Theory for two reasons.

First, I began this writing as a reply to an article about the Just War Theory in the June 2017 issue of Commonweal. Second, while writing the reply, I found it was impossible to avoid discussing a number of other issues and problems that had to surface in the discussion. It can be said that the other issues and problems come to mind when one learns that the Just War Theory simply does not work anymore. It can no longer be applied to our world for reasons to be given.

What has come to be known as the Just War Theory originated with early Christianity, around the time of St. Augustine of Hippo. He is generally believed to be its author. He is said to have referred to the scriptures as a source for the "Principles" set forth to define a "just" war. Based upon his "Principles," he taught his community that some wars are "just" and others "unjust" in light of the "Principles" he enunciated.

Like all responsible doctrine that has come down to us through the ages, the "Principles" have been refined over time.

St. Thomas Aquinas is said to have revised the "Principles" and to have given us three criteria for a "just" war. Those three criteria are said to be: the war must be fought by a legitimate authority, and the wars must be fought for a just reason or cause, and they must be fought for the right motive or intention.

Like all authentic Catholic doctrine, our understanding of the issues evolves and deepens over time, up to and including today. That is why what has come down to us today appears to involve no fewer than seven principles. They are:

1. Last Resort-A just war can only be waged after all peaceful options are considered. Force can only be used as a last resort.

2. Legitimate Authority- A just war can only be waged by a legitimate authority. Individuals or sub-groups within a society cannot take it upon themselves to go to war.

3. Just Cause-A just war can only be waged for an injustice that has already been inflicted upon the nation or country going to war. The objective of going to war can only be to somehow correct the wrong that has been done.

4. Probable Success-A just war can only be waged when it is likely or probable that the warring country will succeed in its efforts. If there is no serious likelihood that a so-called "just" war can be won, the war itself cannot be said to be "just."

5. Right Intention-A just war can only be fought to bring about peace. Peace must be the objective of going to war.

6. Proportionality-The violence undertaken must be proportionate to the violence inflicted by the aggressor. It cannot exceed the level of violence inflicted and cannot be disproportionate to the casualties suffered.

7. Civilian Casualties-The warring parties must make a distinction between soldiers and nonmilitary personnel. The warring parties must always avoid killing civilians. The death of civilians is only justified when they are unavoidable such as an attack on a military target.

It should be noted that the authors who have continued to write about the Just War Theory have distinguished between two different sets of criteria. They are said to be "jus ad bellum," or the "justice of going to war," and "jus in bello," the justice or the ethics with which a war is fought. Since St. Augustine and St. Aquinas, the world has undergone many changes, and it continues to undergo many more at an even faster pace. That is why we would do well to review the writings of more recent experts in the area of the Just War Theory.

Perhaps one starting point is Michael Walzer's book entitled "Just and Unjust Wars." I suppose some Catholic authors would disapprove of this book because I think Mr. Walzer seems to basically accept war as a possibly unavoidable reality of human history; something that is not going to go away very soon. But I chose his book specifically because he argues "both sides" of the issue in the sense that he provides theories and reviews actual historical events while analyzing the morality of conflicts.

He writes about what constitutes "the crime" of war. He writes about the morality of certain military tactics, and the rules of war. He writes about "aggression" as opposed to "intervention," while acknowledging that one can easily be disguised as the other. He writes about noncombatant immunity, and military necessity.

He talks to us about the moral dilemmas involving guerilla warfare, and terrorism (see principle number two above). All of the so-called "pros and cons" are well discussed. But then, something else happens; something very timely. He reaches the topic of nuclear war. And it is nuclear war that may have finally rendered war itself obsolete.

In writing about the nuclear issue, Mr. Walzer reviews the real possibility of nuclear war, and he definitely asserts that it simply cannot be done. I cannot recall ever having asked anyone what they think they would experience if their community became the target of nuclear weapons, but I know I have tried to imagine the event. Consistent with my terrible fantasy, the most effective language I have ever read about nuclear war was a statement published by Physicians for Social Responsibility during the nuclear arms race of the nineteen-eighties. At a convention in San Francisco, they published the statement that, in effect, said, "If we continue to [stockpile nuclear armaments], we will bring about the first catastrophe in human history in which the survivors will envy the dead." That said it all for me and my "terrible fantasy." But then he treats "nuclear deterrence" in a very special way, and for a very special reason to be explained. When Mr. Walzer reaches the topic of "nuclear deterrence," he writes:

> A new kind of war was born at Hiroshima and what we were given was a first glimpse of its deadliness. Though fewer people were killed than in the fire-bombing of Tokyo, they were killed with monstrous ease. One plane, one bomb, with such a weapon. Atomic was death indeed, indiscriminate and total, and after Hiroshima, the first task of political leaders everywhere was to prevent its recurrence.

Here I don't take Mr. Walzer to be comparing the "pros and cons" of nuclear war. I read him taking a distinct stand against even the most minute risk of it ever occurring again. He goes on to discuss the blatant immorality of something that we, as Catholics, are all participating in today; nuclear deterrence:

> The question is a difficult one. It has generated in the years since Hiroshima a significant body of literature exploring the relation between nuclear deterrence and just war. This has been the work mostly of theologians and philosophers, but some of the strategists of deterrence have also been involved; they worry about the act of terrorizing as much as conventional soldiers worry about the act of killing.

John Bennett is then quoted:

> . . . how can a nation live with its conscience. . . and know that it is preparing to kill twenty million children in another nation if the worst should come to the worst?" Then Walzer says "the immorality lies in the threat itself.[1]

---

1. Walzer, *Just and Unjust Wars*, 289

Mr. Walzer is talking about nuclear deterrence, not nuclear war. That is to say, the threat of nuclear war is in and of itself an overwhelming moral issue, and not one that can any longer be acceptable.

Here also we may have at least two examples of art imitating life. In the movie "Crimson Tide," two American naval officers are aboard an American nuclear submarine. They are discussing nuclear war when the young officer played by Denzel Washington suggests that, in the nuclear age, the "enemy" is war itself. The Captain of the ship, played by Gene Hackman, appears to scoff at the idea. As in real life, and probably more frequently than we realize, a nuclear mishap almost occurs.

In another movie called "War Games," a computer is entrusted with performing the sequence of electronic maneuvers that, when so commanded, will ultimately launch nuclear missiles in the direction of the Soviet Union. As in real life, a human mistake is made and the computer, ultimately learned to be named "Joshua" undertakes the task of preparing to launch the missiles. For one reason or another, a heroic young man (Matthew Broderick) engages "Joshua" in the game of tic tac to in order to preclude the launch. "Joshua" is ultimately prevented from launching because he is unable to win the game of tic tac to after having exhausted all of the possible tic tac to moves on the computer screen. The computer system disallows the launch as "Joshua" declares; "An interesting game. The only winning move is not to play." Why do the authors of our fiction have to tell us what we are really doing?

As to our Catholic faith, one final statement about nuclear deterrence is to be made, and this is not fictional. It is not even theoretical. One vocal body on the issue of the nuclear arms race for many years has been the U.S. Catholic Bishops. On May 3, 1983 at the height of the cold war, they wrote and circulated "The Challenge of Peace: God's Promise and Our Response; A Pastoral Letter on War and Peace by the National Council of Catholic Bishops."

They therein stated that a nation may stockpile nuclear weapons, but only as part of a "transitional strategy" in which an effort to pursue arms control and disarmament was being conducted. Sadly, the U.S. today is "modernizing" its nuclear arsenal (as if regressing was modernizing). In a current editorial circulated by one newspaper, today's group of U.S. Bishops is quoted as recently saying that because the U.S. is no longer ". . .moving with full determination to nuclear disarmament, the 'thin moral acceptance' the bishops once gave to U.S. deterrence has outlived itself." I.e., there is no longer a great distinction between "possessing" nuclear arms and "using" nuclear arms. The nuclear weapons must go. This appears to be consistent with Michael Walzer's appraisal of the morality of nuclear deterrence.

In his book "Isaiah," Daniel Berrigan, S.J. treats the hackneyed nature of the Just War theory. He writes:

> War, any war, erupts. Shortly there-after the "moral theologians" enter and the just-war nonsense is dusted off. With a great spasm of casuistry, the war is forced and fitted to the Procrustean theory. Swords are vindicated again, even as they kill.[2]

2. Berrigan, *Isaiah*, 13

2

Fear and Backlash

PEACE, JUSTICE, FEAR, AND BACKLASH

Having read Dr. Gerald W. Schlabach's article in the June 2017 edition of Commonweal about the Just War Theory, I attempted to write a reply based upon my limited experiences with Peace and Justice organizations in several Catholic parishes in which I have lived. My effort at keeping that reply brief proved futile for the main reason that for the most part, the Just War Theory is a Peace and Justice issue. Therefore, the Just War Theory cannot be discussed absent discussing many other peace and justice topics; they are several in number and cannot be avoided.

The first unavoidable topic is the backlash that occurs when peace and justice issues are raised in the setting of comfortable suburban parishes. Many Peace and Justice encounters necessarily flow from any attempted, honest discussion about the Just War Theory. With all due respect to the experts on the Just War Theory, I cannot imagine how the Just War Theory can be discussed in isolation for the simple reason that its applicability to the modern world has become, at the very least, doubtful, and probably impossible.

The modern world onto which some would attempt to apply the Just War Theory is much more intricate than its earliest proponents could have ever imagined, especially with its modern weaponry. Any attempt at effectively applying the Just War Theory to our modern world would be catastrophic. Even to entertain its application invites the catastrophe.

What matters in terms of the content of any contemporary reading of the Just War Theory is much less important than the nature of the civilization to which it is applied. Augustine of Hippo would have had an impossible task before him if he were attempting to apply the Just War Theory to the nuclear age.

After the Nonviolence and Just Peace conference in Rome, Dr. Schlabach writes "what's wrong with the Just War Theory?" He then explains that, at its close, the conference ". . .issued an appeal to the Catholic Church, urging that it recommit to the centrality of Gospel nonviolence."

But how does one ". . .appeal to the Catholic Church" and to whom should the "appeal" be directed? Does one "appeal" to the Catholic Church by writing to a distant prelate about peace, justice, and Gospel nonviolence knowing that such a prelate's esoteric words, even if published, will never be read by the people for whom this book is written? Does one "appeal" to local parish clergy about peace and justice vis-a-vis the Just War Theory only to be humored? Every peace and justice activist promptly learns that in the case of comfortable suburban middle-class parishes, local parish clergy dare not challenge their congregations to revisit their political world views.

This is especially true in the case of militarism and the dark side of capitalism. These are the types of issues that invoke the parish "backlash" to be described. Challenging that kind of congregation to revisit those issues, Gospel non-violence and inescapably the Just War Theory, could easily lead to the removal and professional suicide for any priest or pastor. I recall having conversations with several parish priests during the nineteen eighties about peace and justice issues. One pastor, while agreeing with me on a peace and justice issue and who could only be described as "well situated" and "very popular" told me that he knew he would be "instantly removed" if he spoke out against militarism.

In another case, one pastor told me he agreed with me on a peace and justice issue but did not wish to be "transferred to Nome, Alaska" if he spoke out about any peace and justice issue that was contrary to his parishioners' political or social world view. That is why it is evident that only a "laity to laity" interaction has any chance of bringing the Just War Theory and the practical consequences of its attempted application to the table in parish life. In the case of many Catholics, it would be the first time in their lives that the futility of a Church doctrine such as the Just War Theory would be placed before them.

As an aside, one often hears the objection that activists should "keep politics out of religion," or that reflexive objection about a "separation of church and state." The problem with these objections is that they have become meaningless over the centuries due to the reality of cultural evolution.

That is because Jesus preached His message to a largely "one-on-one" world; a world in which most men built their own homes, grew their own crops, and tended and slaughtered their own livestock. They manufactured most if not all of their own tools and clothing, and even delivered or assisted in the delivery of their own children. A few tasks were performed for them by those who had the wherewithal to perform them, such as making their wine, and perhaps manufacturing tents and iron tools.

Jesus' message was couched in terms of a one-on-one world and His lessons offered were spoken to His listeners in terms of how one individual is called to treat another. But as permanent and basic as His lessons are, they must now be applied to the world we have erected. As time went on, fewer and fewer people remained "jacks of all trades" and we allowed one another to limit ourselves to specific tasks. One man made tools, another built homes, and others farmed. We came to that place in history in which almost all of us specialized. It remains true that we are still called today to a "one-on-one" ethic as to how we are to treat the individuals around us. We still have neighbors, friends, spouses, children, and siblings. But for the most part, large social and business entities perform the tasks that centuries ago, we each performed in and for our own households. In short, having specialized, we created a world in which we now do things both FOR and TO one another through institutions; specifically, corporate and government bureaucracies. We are not called to rethink the Gospel, but we are called to rethink its application.

The question used to be "what will my conduct do to or for this or that person?" The question has become more complex; "what will my support for this group, agency, corporation, or government bureaucracy do to my fellow human beings and the world in which we all must live?" And as for staying out of politics", what many of us seem to really want is a harmless church; a church that will not only avoid difficult topics, but a church that will tell us only what we want to hear. In a book containing a series of diary entries and homilies by Archbishop Saint Oscar Romero, who was murdered for confronting the violence by his own Salvadoran government against his congregations, he states on April 6, 1978:

> A church that does not provoke crisis, a gospel that
> does not disturb, a word of God that does not rankle,
> a word of God that does not touch the concrete sin of
> the society in which it is being proclaimed—what kind
> of Gospel is that?[1]

From time to time, I hear someone in the "holiness business" declare, using what has come to be known as "code speak", "we never talk about politics." Given the reality of "code speak," like any translation from one language to another, I hear that person say "I insist on keeping my harmless church. Give me piety, and let's call it holiness."

But decades earlier, another Catholic, Dorothy Day, while on the road to canonization proclaimed that we measure our discipleship by the amount of trouble we are in.

We all know the names of many bishops and archbishops. We all know the names of many people who became leaders in social

---

1. Romero, *The Scandal of Redemption*, p. 54

movements. How do we explain the fact that the archbishop who calls for a "church that provokes crisis" is now canonized? How is it that a woman who recognized the military industrial complex as being the "sinkhole" for our tax dollars that it is, is the one who is on the road to canonization, first being called a "servant of God?" How welcome would Oscar Romero or Dorothy Day be to speak in our comfortable, suburban parishes today?

Back to the question Dr. Schlabach implies; how does a peace and justice organization bring the Just War Theory and its practical "consequences" before their parish? Does that organization try to schedule talks on the parish grounds and announce its purpose to the laity? If that is not permitted, and often times it is not, does a peace and justice organization confront their own parishioners in a church parking lot after Mass about the Just War Theory and peace and nonviolence in general only to be viewed with contempt, disdain, and ridicule for being "unpatriotic?"

I witnessed events of that nature during the 1980s, and the peace and justice organization's members did in fact incur the wrath of their priests and laity.

Is a peace and justice organization to hope that somehow, the number of adherents to their message in their parish will reach a fraction of the number of their parishioners' numerical "tipping point" needed to effect change? It is doubtful that that will occur, given the level of resistance within the Catholic laity. I witnessed events of that nature during the 1980s, and the peace and justice organization's members did incur the wrath and fear of their priests and their parishioners. That is what real peace and justice activists actually do and experience somewhere in the Catholic parishes of the U.S. every day.

Dr. Schlabach realizes that not only must revisiting the Just War Theory and its issues be done in a "laity to laity" manner, but he knows what forces will promptly resist the efforts of peace activists in their parishes. He writes that we are ". . .a populace formed in habits of fear, seduced by nationalism, trained to rely on military actions for easy solutions, and easily swayed by false leaders or so-called Just War Theory and its concomitant issues facilitates the fear and nationalism complained of.

Is the Church in its present state structurally capable of the "Gospel Nonviolence" referenced in Dr. Schlabach's article?

By way of explanation, I recall an incident that occurred in my parish years ago that remains vivid in my memory today. I and a few other parishioners formed a Pax Christi chapter and announced our first meeting in the parish bulletin. That alone was a very difficult thing to do. The pastor at first objected that "Pax Christi is not an organization that is approved by the Archdiocese." But somehow, the Pax Christi meeting occurred. The issues were discussed in the context of U.S. intervention in Central America, and nonviolence and peacemaking were the obvious topics.

After the meeting ended and only the organizers were present, a young priest entered the hall and asked us for a "count"; how many people attended? There was no reference to the truth of Pax Christi's message or the content of the discussion; just how many people came? His inquiry is easily translated into more "code speak": "Is this something the customers want to hear?"

This is not just a criticism of the type of "training" or "education" our parish priests are getting. More importantly, it is a scathing criticism of what I suspect that we have done to them. They study for years and then are ordained to bring the Eucharist before us, and they do. But seminary training is very thorough, and one can only infer the implied mandate to "avoid" challenging the laity to rethink its world view.

Something is evident. In the largely middle-class suburban parishes, as soon as the newly ordained priest is assigned to his first parish, it is made very clear to him that there are certain topics or "issues" that are "off limits." These are typically the issues and problems which our so-called "Just War Theory" serves to perpetuate. These are typically the issues that our peace and justice activists try to address. As long as the Church functions like a sales organization "pleasing her customers" the message of nonviolence will fall on deaf ears if the parishioners do not want their political world view challenged. That is the type of suburban congregations that are made up of "customers" who must be "pleased" at all costs by the "sales department."

I typed and framed a statement and hung it on my wall. It reads:

> Only a true friend would challenge us to rethink our world view. A lazy contemporary would not believe we were worth it.

I recall a conversation I had with a parish priest about the omnipresent correlate to "Just War" problems; nationalism. I met him by accident in a market near the church, and as we sat down to enjoy our lunch, I mentioned that I was uncomfortable with the level of nationalism I sensed among the parishioners. He was quick to tell me that "nationalism" is never preached from the pulpit. Subtleties and nuances are important here. He also said by implication that the evils of nationalism are never preached about either. In "Isaiah", Daniel Berrigan calls this "conniving silence."

Some of the parish priests of our largely comfortable suburban parishes are masters at it. The American flag is revered and (I would argue) almost worshiped in the parish hall during different presentations. The military becomes a fetish when military service members visit or speak at events. Father stands by silently and watches, smiles approvingly, and the American flag is permitted to serve as the parish's moral compass. Again, Father Daniel Berrigan's conniving silence.

Literate, thinking Catholics should realize that once their country finds itself in a perpetual state of war to the point at which our national economy cannot function without it, something has gone wrong. When one discusses these issues with a parishioner, something typical occurs. The person looks at the ground, mutters something dismissive, (usually something about "human nature") and the conversation ends. At best, a few of us simply throw up our hands in resignation at the realization that we are being "played" by the government.

Many of us seem to suspect that many of the international "incidents" used to justify our going to war are "engineered." In fact, with the "information age," it is even more easily achieved, and we are even more easily misled. Contrived lies about "weapons of mass destruction" are only the "tip of the iceberg." We are now knowingly living in a war machine; it is becoming our national livelihood. The Catholic population of the United States rarely, if ever talks about the military industrial complex. But the military industrial complex is actually BECOMING our government, and our perpetual state of war is maintained largely because of the unimaginable amounts of money that change hands daily.

Many Catholics in the more comfortable suburban parishes are actually employed by it, either directly or indirectly, and I am certain that in many cases, they were originally enticed by their salaries and actually believed in the complete legitimacy of their nation state. Any one of us can be lured into believing that we are somehow "morally superior" to the "other." Therefore, several Catholics have related to me that the weaponry they design and manufacture poses no moral problem for them, as long as it serves to protect an "American" life. The consequence to the "other" is of lesser importance, even if they are women and children being mutilated by our drones.

It would appear that the divided loyalty between the Body of Christ and the nation state is so omnipresent and so chronic and so deeply embedded among the Catholic population that it is going virtually unnoticed. That divided loyalty consists of nothing less than the United States of America versus the Body of Christ; they can never be one and the same, but for some, they appear to have become so in their minds. We cannot be who we claim we are until we do what we claim to be. So, clichés aside, how does one "appeal to the Catholic Church?"

Oftentimes when a controversy rages on for a great deal of time, it is because the same arguments have been made over and over again in the absence of some more new relevant input. If that is true, then something new must be introduced to move the argument along; the argument being the nation-state versus the Body of Christ. In the same way, Dr. Schlabach also makes it clear that the arguments centering on the Just War Theory have been going on for centuries. Is it possible that there is a Power or a

Force behind the disconnect between who we are and what we do? Perhaps there is, and I would like to discuss that Power or Force in a later chapter. Perhaps the "input" needed to move the issues along is "input" regarding that Power or Force. But before we can talk about that Power or Force the discussion has to follow our sequence of issues that have rendered the Just War Theory obsolete. The first phenomenon that logically follows that renders the Just War Theory obsolete is the phenomenon known as "Nationalism."

3

Nationalism

"I PLEDGE ALLEGIANCE TO. . . . . WHAT?"

RECALL THAT DR. SCHLABACH writes that much of the ". . .just-war discourse" will do [little] to curtail warfare or create conditions of peace when a populace (or a parish, for that matter) is formed in habits of fear, seduced by nationalism, trained to rely on military actions for easy solutions, and easily swayed by false leaders or misleading popular passions." All of these issues, "fear," "passions," etc. are included in nationalism.

Before even discussing nationalism as "the problem" one must understand that "nationalism" and "patriotism" are not one and the same thing. Some confusion must be dispelled. Although definitions of the two overlap, the differences between the two are greater. It will be helpful to examine the two terms here. Webster's dictionary defines "patriotism" as being:

> Love and loyal or zealous support of one's own country, especially in all matters involving other countries; nationalism

Nationalism, on the other hand, is defined as:

Devotion to one's own nation; Excessive patriotism 'narrow,' (my emphasis) or jingoist patriotism; Chauvinism. The doctrine that national interests, security, etc. are more important than international; opposed to internationalism, etc.

The difference between the two words is easily seen. When one contemplates both the singularity of the world that Jesus saved and the fact that it is becoming smaller, the word "selfish" becomes synonymous with nationalism. Let's risk an adult conversation about the difference between patriotism and nationalism by talking about both.

I have never even attempted to talk about either the Just War Theory or nonviolence at the national level without raising the topic of nationalism. That is for the simple reason that sane responsible patriotism aside, nationalism is national violence. When a people (or their parish) make a conscious decision to ignore or oppose any local, national or international effort at even attempting to protect the earth, that is nationalism. That is, to use an ugly phrase, "flag worship." Jesus cannot be part of that picture. When a people (or their parish) consciously and willingly engage in warfare for decades on end without even questioning whether or not their policies might be counterproductive, let alone addictive, that is nationalism. That is, to use an ugly phrase, "flag worship." Jesus cannot be part of that picture. When a people (or their parish) say "my country above all other people," that is nationalism. That is, to use an ugly phrase, "flag worship." Jesus cannot be part of that picture. When a people (or their parish) say "my country, right or wrong, my country," in the complete absence of any moral premise, that is nationalism. That is, to use an ugly phrase, "flag worship." Jesus cannot be part of that picture.

In the alternative, when a people (or their parish) work to protect natural resources from pollution, that is patriotism. That is love of country. That is a desire to make it better. When a people (or their parish) work to protect, let alone save the earth from being defaced by strip mining and unregulated fossil fuel extraction, that is patriotism. That is love of country. That is a desire to make it better. When a people work to build and maintain equally cared for public school systems for every part of the community, that is patriotism. That is love of country. That is a desire to make it better. When a people (or their parish) work to protect their forests and wildlife from indiscriminate destruction, that is patriotism. That is love of country. That is a desire to make it better. When a people (or a parish) call for health care for everyone, calls for making health care a right as opposed to a privilege, that is patriotism. That is love of country. That is a desire to make it better. When a people (or a parish) raise concerns about decade upon decade of massive military spending in the absence of any plausible explanation as to why, that is patriotism. That is love of country. That is a desire to make it better. One might even surmise that "love of country" begins with "love of community" and by definition, all of the people in it.

I recall attending choir practice in the home of a parish music minister. We took a break from practicing and one way or another, the topics of the American flag and Jesus came up in conversation. I must have suggested that the two should not be confused, and a lady in our choir uttered "well, they're both the same thing!!!" I'm certain she did not understand the import of what she had just said, but in effect, she had "said it all." A national symbol had taken on the air of the holy. ("Power" or "Force" to be discussed later).

I also recall something much more disturbing. I was browsing through a set of television programs and I incidentally stopped at and watched part of a televangelist show. The orchestra was playing a "patriotic" hymn, and bibles were on display everywhere, flying and waving in the air. A close-up was made of a woman, bible in hand, with tears streaming down her face. She was gazing mesmerized at the stage because a giant red, white and blue American flag was being hoisted into the air, all in the context of "worshiping Jesus." I am certain that the real nature of that event never crossed the mind of that lady or the congregation that was so enthralled by their American flag, but we have already used the phrase "flag worship" for a reason. Our first topic was the Just War

Theory. It is definitely time to talk about nationalism as opposed to patriotism, soon to be followed by other related topics.

As discussed, in Webster's Dictionary, the definitions of patriotism and nationalism overlap, but only slightly. Webster defines patriotism as "love and loyal or zealous support of one's own country, especially in all matters involving other countries." Webster goes on to define nationalism in a similar manner, but with an important, and for our purposes, an even insidious difference. With Webster's, nationalism is defined as ". . .devotion to one's nation; patriotism. Excessive narrow, or jingoistic patriotism; chauvinism, the doctrine that national interests, security, etc. are more important than international considerations. . ." The important point is that for the purpose of this writing, when we meet people whose hearts and minds are engulfed by nationalism, we meet people for whom right and wrong are defined by the state!!!

For example, the Gospel may call us to "embrace the foreigner" or to be a "good Samaritan" to those fleeing for their lives from tyrannical governments and failed economies. But with nationalism, governments often define the "fleeing poor" as being "illegal" if not "dangerous" human beings. The important point to be made *here is that, with nationalism, and mandates the valuing or the devaluing of human* beings. The state defines how we are to treat the air and the water, while the state demands the reverence depicted in our woman at the televangelist's event. The state determines who we are to kill, absent any credible explanation as to why.

Those parishes engulfed by nationalism often find themselves unable to question the state. We are called to assume we are being told the truth regarding our issues and our decisions. Nationalism demands that we do so with uncritical obedience. Many "Catholic" parishes fall in line. It does not require too great a leap in logic to see that the state wants to serve as the functional deity in our lives. Again, for this reason, our "Power" or "Force" will become a topic for a later chapter.

But modernly, the state cannot trick us into falling prey to nationalistic idolatry without the employment of religious symbols. Hence, our lady at the televangelist event. Pairing religious and national symbols in the context of parish worship is only the beginning of a phenomenon that at least approaches idolatry. Flag worship at the national level, with that parish's support, follows.

But this is also where the ultimate cowardice occurs. Catholic men and women will quickly interrupt and cry "but that is your opinion. In my opinion, these are the right things to do. We have always supported these institutions. This is how my parish has always lived." Faced with the reality of murderous nationalism, Catholic men and women and their pastors quickly object with cowardice. "I do not share your opinion," is the omnipresent excuse. No alternate argument is presented. No justification for their position is offered. One only hears "I do not agree with you, period." Faced with these issues, they only attempt to bury their cowardice in their own noise. Senator Daniel Patrick Moynihan taught us how to approach a controversy with both humility and bravery when he said we are all entitled to our own opinions, but we cannot mandate our own facts.

Faced with the reality of what is being done with their tax dollars, and the evidence thereof, those same men and women and their pastors have an important decision to make.

"IMAGINED COMMUNITIES"

A Good Book on Nationalism

Benedict Anderson writes an excellent book tracing the origin (very recent in human history) of nationalism. His book "Imagined Communities" was one book I chose to use largely because of its title. I have always intended to argue that there is something illusory about this entity we revere called "the country." I have made an honest effort to determine what this entity known as "the country" or "the nation" actually consists of. While trying to learn what aspect of it is real, if any, it seemed to me to be of primary importance to state what it is not. Then, and only then, will we be equipped to see beyond the illusory aspects of the "nation" or the "country" or the "Imagined Community" if you will, to view the tangible institutions masquerading as "our country."

Anderson goes straight to the heart of the matter early in Chapter Two of his book. After writing about how nationalism gradually replaced the monarchs and dynasties of the world, he writes about what he would probably call a symbol of the new "nations" that followed. As an example, he writes about tombs of the unknown soldiers. He writes about how the tombs of unknown soldiers are given a reverence and "ghostly national imaginings." But more importantly, there is an aura of death yet immortality about them, and he sees a ". . .strong affinity with religious imaginings." He seems to mean that the "tombs of the unknown soldiers" seem to serve as holy references to "holy institutions" or "countries."

In his book, he depicts how, as nationalism began to develop, individual men and women began to "imagine" themselves as being somehow connected to one another, largely through a common vernacular language. Anderson would argue that as the older "divine right of kings" gave way to nationalism.

The holiness once attributed to one's king became a form of secularized holiness attributed to one's nation. People began killing and dying for it, and therefore, it became all the holier. Hence, the holiness of the tomb of the unknown soldier. The logic seemed to be that if someone would die for it, it must in fact be holy. Yet at this point, we have to be reminded that the nation remained an imagined community. It remained an imagined set of relationships.

For our purposes, a counterbalance must be introduced. Although the nation state is an imagined set of relationships, the Body of Christ is not. This is our issue.

It is easy to feel the annoyance one experiences at considering the possibility that something we have "believed in" all of our lives might not actually be there. The reader is asked to be patient. It must be conceded that there is something tangible "out there" being called "the country," but we owe it to ourselves to determine what it might actually be.

Other authors write that nationalism is a collective state of mind. All of the authors emphasize the ethereal nature of the nation, and many warn us that nationalism wields the power that it has over our minds today specifically because nationalism remains unexamined and its assumptions unchallenged. We, as Catholics, with the benefit of the Prophets and two thousand years of revelation and theologizing, surely should be capable of a thoughtful, cautious breaking of the spell of the phenomenon of nationalism.

If the nation is simply an imagined set of relationships, what tangible entities are out there demanding our allegiance, our lives, our sons' lives, even the kind of religious fervor described for us by Benedict Anderson?

Admittedly, we have looked at a very unsettling idea; the possibility that the nation state, the country, if you will, is a virtual illusion. We have done so with the help of a secular author who serves as an historian. But for our purposes as Catholics, perhaps, we owe it to ourselves to examine the same issue through the eyes of a Catholic author. Then we can probably be a little more confident in our argument.

We have looked at the nation state and examined the possibility that it is in actuality an imagined community. By imagined community we mean that as a singular political or social entity, it may not be what we would otherwise call real. We pledge our allegiance to it, and many Catholics define themselves as individuals by identifying with it. But for our purposes, if the nation state is not a tangible entity, how did we come to make such an error in logic? It may or may not be sufficient to merely excuse ourselves by saying that we were taught to identify ourselves as Americans, or Frenchmen, or Englishmen etc. But therein lies the problem. Has our having identified ourselves with a particular nation state actually served to obscure our real identity as God's own children? I would argue that it does.

The very word "nation" must be carefully examined. No one can count the number of Christians who have distorted the biblical term "nation" to accommodate their political obsessions or their world views. Thinking Christians realize that the biblical use of the word "nation" is a reference to a racial or tribal or spiritual entity known as the Israel of the Old Testament, certainly not a modern political entity known as the Israel or the nation-state of Israel of today. Similarly, and tragically, we probably will always have among us those Catholics (and their parishes) who insist that their country is a "nation" that has been "raised up" to demonstrate to the world how life is to be lived.

TEILHARD

An All-encompassing Catholicism

There is available to us another specifically Catholic author who also "immensely" served the world in ways that have not yet been counted because he served us not only as a theologian, but as a scientist. It seems he teaches us how our real identity is to be determined by literally circumventing the nation state in order to learn who we really are. He has also served us immensely because, as is the case with all authentic prophets, he lived well ahead of his time. Further, when one reads about Teilhard's life, one realizes that we did to Teilhard what we do to all prophets; we punish them severely for telling us what we would rather not hear.

Pere Teilhard de Chardin was a brilliant Jesuit Paleontologist who lived during the first half of the twentieth century. In his book "The Divine Milieu," he explains how he developed a very deep understanding of salvation history by beginning first with the understanding that the world and the universe are not simply made of matter. He was able to glean from the scriptures and from scientific observation that all matter is slowly evolving into spirit. This is obviously a gross over-simplification, and the readers owe it to themselves to read "The Divine Milieu." Through his theology of evolution (and he did not allow the word to frighten him) he came to realize that the entire planet is "converging" towards what he called the "Omega Point," (a term borrowed from Revelations 22:13); that point in human history in which the human community and, by extension, each one of us outgrows nationalism and all other petty identities and merges into that state called the Pleroma in which the Parousia, Jesus's Second Coming, becomes possible.

Rather than trying to review his entire book, and in order to avoid misquoting Fr. Teilhard, I have chosen to quote a spokesperson for the American Teilhard Association's website, Louis Savary. I asked the Association for an opinion on my understanding of Teilhard's position on nationalism, and Mr. Savary replied:

> Teilhard would say that humanity and earth are already one giant organism, physically and biologically. Humans are slowly realizing that they are also one giant mind, since we are already totally connected worldwide through the media. . .Some nations, like the United States, and most of Europe, realize that, though they are unique as nations with their own languages and cultures and customs, they are all citizens of one world. people of these nations hear of famines or plagues happening far from their homeland, they respond with appropriate heart-felt concern for them and offer practical assistance. . . Teilhard might note that not everyone in every nation has a global consciousness. We are not yet at what scientists call a "tipping point," where the vast majority of the human race in every nation shares this GLOBAL CONSCIOUSNESS, (my emphasis), but we are approaching that point. (I would only add that a few of us who are deeply plagued with nationalism resist the process vehemently). I think Teilhard would not support the kind of extreme nationalism where the people of that nation were convinced that they were the only important nation in the world and that they should have concern for no one but themselves; where no other lives or concerns are valuable or significant except their own lives and welfare.[1]

We are all ultimately, with our own individual personal identities, "merging with the Pleroma," as is the collective human community. In the grand scheme of things, the nation state plays no role in our salvation. We are, and will always be, God's children alone. Perhaps we are now called to learn that the next major "shift" or "growth spurt" for the human community will be the

---

1. Savary, A Paraphrasing of Teilhard de Chardin, The American Teilhard Assn.

relative insignificance of the nation state. Regarding Fr. Teilhard, if the word "Catholic" is to be interpreted as "universal", tell me who the real Catholic is.

When I think back over the conversations I have had (or attempted) with many people over nationalism, I recall two very basic features of their state of mind. The first feature is that their unquestioned loyalty to the nation was an emotion. Their emotional attachment to their nation was and is a feeling, an unquestioned form of allegiance rooted solely in their emotional makeup. That is why symbols of the nation state are so important to understanding the power of nationalism. Symbols take the form of the flag, and often dramatic and so-called "patriotic" music such as one hears from a "big brass band," although we have discussed the difference between nationalism and patriotism.

As Benedict Anderson writes, the real power of nationalism lies in the fact that it has gone on without being analyzed for so many years. The second important thing to be noticed is that data, information, facts, if you will, do not enter into the experience of nationalism. It remains an emotion totally divorced from thought or analysis.

Regarding the second feature of nationalism, we are brought to another very important faith-related observation, yet an observation regarding the crucial importance of "thought and analysis" as opposed to our "precious feelings." It involves a faith-related observation that many of us have virtually overlooked. It has everything to do with the injection of "thought and analysis" into our faith experience. I will draw from the scriptures to make the point. Let us look to the twenty-fourth chapter of the gospel of Luke.

It begins with the first Easter Sunday.

> On the same day, two of them were going to a village named Emmaus, about seven miles from Jerusalem, and they were talking to each other about all the things that had happened. As they discussed, Jesus himself drew near, and walked along with them; they saw him, but somehow did not him. Jesus said to them 'what are you talking about, back and forth, as you walk along? They

stood still, with sad faces. One of them, named Cleopas, asked him, "Are you the only man living in Jerusalem who does not know what has been happening these last few days?" "What things," Jesus asked.

Then Cleopas and his companion (perhaps his wife, as some scholars suggest) relate to Jesus, still unrecognized, all of the things (now contained in the scriptures) regarding Jesus' passion and death and then they report about the empty tomb reported by "some women" in their company. Then comes my favorite part of the New Testament. Jesus says to Cleopas and his companion:

> How foolish you are. How slow you are to believe everything the prophets said! Was it not necessary for the Messiah to suffer these things and enter into His glory?[2]

I have always felt compelled to paraphrase this passage. I have always heard Jesus saying something like the following sentences regarding emotions verses thought:

> Yes, the scriptures call you to a change of heart, but you are still expected to think. The Father has given you the capacity, the requirement to feel, but you are still expected to think."

That is the challenge before us today. For me, this passage goes directly to the problem of nationalism. Flags and brass bands overrun our hearts, but while stepping back and examining our loyalties, the Gospel requires us to think, just as Jesus required his disciples to think on the road to Emmaus. Cleopas and his companion almost missed the point. They didn't sufficiently study the Scriptures.

Staying with the Scriptures for a while, there is another Gospel passage that I suspect is relevant for the question of nationalism. We again try to discern exactly what nationalism means when compared to what the Gospel requires of us. When Jesus is quoted in John 8:44, something descriptive occurs that I suspect some of us have allowed to go unnoticed. When John's Gospel tells us that

---

2. Luke, *New Revised Standard Version*, 24:13–19, 25–26

Satan is "a murderer and a liar from the beginning," Jesus is typically taken to have given us two very descriptive signs of Satan's presence in our world; not in "The Garden," but in our world. Many of the scriptural writers that I have read recently discuss "the Fall" as if it were a singular event occurring in Genesis. But a careful reading should lead us to understand that the "Fall" is an on-going process among us and in our world.

Here is Satan's process of victimization through "murdering" and "lying." Being on-going, this process consists of on-going events occurring in the here and now in our lifetimes. To understand the relevance of John 8:44 to our lives, we must perform two tasks. First, we must accept the fact that Satan is alive and well in our world and that his "lying and murdering" continues. Let us carefully look at the phrase "a liar and a murderer from the beginning." "Lying" and "murdering" occur in the same context and within the same phrase. Does that not imply that the "murdering" is a direct consequence of the "lying?" Find the lie, and the murdering follows.

Because we continue to live in that fallen world in which Satan's "lying" and "murdering" continues, our second task as thinking Catholics becomes the task of identifying the "lying" and the "murdering." I would argue that there is no greater and more widespread example of a "lie" giving rise to consequent "murder" than nationalism and its consequent warfare. We have already tried to carefully analyze nationalism and found it to be largely reduced to the reverence given to a war machine. The subsequent carnage can easily be seen as the "murdering" that follows the "lie" of nationalism.

We love to say "God so loved the world. . ." But how far does "our world" really go? Does nationalism allow us to see a "world," or does it merely allow us to see our so-called "country?" To see the singularity of the world, one must look beyond his horizons, or rather his borders, and to think. We are called to view the planet.

4

The National Security State

THE MILITARY INDUSTRIAL COMPLEX

LOOKING BEHIND THE VEIL of the "Country," we find The Big Business of War; Many Catholic parishes look on with smiling approval as our government goes into a very dark business.

"I pledge allegiance to. . . . . . . .Who?"

It isn't difficult to write about the military industrial complex. The challenge lies in the fact that the military industrial complex is largely a perversion of that "imagined community" we used to call the "nation" or the "country" if you will. By that it is meant that earlier, not only did many Catholic Americans fall prey to nationalistic fervor as opposed to a responsible attentiveness to their government and its conduct, they were "looking the other way" while their government became something very different. A "process" occurred.

Whether recent or in the distant past, our legislators learned that when our citizens went to war, their emotional state became such that it was relatively easy to distract them from the manner in which our war time affairs were being conducted. That is, when we went to war, there was money to be made; huge sums of money. Not only did excessive sums of money find their way from the legislators into the pockets of the weapons manufacturers, but in return, those weapons manufacturers supported those legislators financially, and reassured their reelections.

Our business community learned how unimaginable sums of money could be found and how easy it was to "purchase" the legislative support needed for both wartime production and, more recently, for remaining on an incessant war footing for monetary reasons. It was a short step to today's incessant warfare, and so now, our addiction has set in. I found a quotation on the internet that says:

> It used to be that weapons were to fight wars. Now, wars are manufactured to sell weapons.

For the purposes of this book, I will use a term our modern-day movie makers use; our government "morphed" into something very different while we were not watching. Some of our Catholic parishes were manipulated into becoming ardent supporters of the "morphed-into" character by looking the other way.

I cannot know exactly when war profiteering began in the United States. That is for historians to say. Perhaps there was some war profiteering engaged in to a limited extent as early as the American Revolution. However, by the time of the American Civil War, it was well documented.

When the Civil War series by Ken Burns was aired on Public Television, one complete episode was dedicated to war profiteering and was entitled "The Age of Shoddy." The story was told about how a particular boot manufacturer sold a supply of boots to the Union Army, and after only limited use by infantry soldiers, the boots quickly disassembled and became useless. When confronted with this nefarious deed, the manufacturer quickly explained that the boots had been intended for use by cavalrymen!!!

This incident was probably not the beginning of war profiteering in the United States. But our military industrial complex followed a little later in our history and it certainly became much more costly in two different and costly ways. First, through "markups" and "cost overrides", large amounts of money were obviously being misappropriated. Secondly, the fact that the war industry literally seized control of our legislature and its spending was an even more costly loss; the loss of our democracy. The weapons manufacturers bought our government.

But what is the military industrial complex? Certainly, most American Catholics have heard of it, but what is it exactly, and what does the phrase "military industrial complex" really mean?

The military industrial complex is that conglomerate of weapons manufacturers, and military purchasers who manufacture and supply goods and weaponry to the United States military, but it is not even that simple. For one thing, by bribing our legislators, the costs of those goods and weapons systems have skyrocketed to the point at which the money paid out by American Catholic taxpayers is inconceivably disproportionate to what is arguably achieved or achievable by them. The other issue not only involves the cost to Catholic taxpayers, but raises the following questions. Has the military industrial complex *actually become* the United States government? Does not the military industrial complex "own and operate" our national legislature and is it not keeping our government functioning in a manner consistent with its own purposes?

For the most part, the federal budget is a matter of public record. But within that maze of figures and expenditures, there is a great deal of spending and intentional waste that can only be described as devious. I reviewed several books on the military industrial complex and the financial burdens it imposes, but I thought the best book that I learned of was entitled "The Pornography of Power" by Robert Scheer. I used Mr. Scheer's book because Mr. Scheer has been reporting on the absurdities of government spending and waste by the military for years. Unfortunately, his book is no longer in print, but he addresses the issue quite well.

Here is a taste of the type of phenomenal waste, if not outright theft, which has been uncovered. In Chapter III, Mr. Scheer writes:

> The business of the military, particularly concerning the expenditure of huge sums of taxpayer money on weapons systems, is by design an opaque subject having more to do with bureaucratic prerogatives and corporate profits than the actual use of those weapons in waging war. There is little enthusiasm among those in the decision-making process for any measure of transparency, which serve no one's interest except the taxpayers who foot the bill. . .Each year, an intricate budget-allocation, a minuet dance of legislators, Pentagon officials, and corporate lobbyists is conducted and largely ignored by the mass media, and therefore the public. This annual ritual matters a great deal in the division of spoils, and it is deliberately shrouded in mystery by its primary practitioners. Only through a rare window, and usually when scandal erupts, do outsiders catch a glimpse of the system's deep corruption.[1]

In Chapter VI Mr. Scheer gives us a lesson in "pork," explaining the meaning of "earmarks" in the federal budget. He names legislators, both Democrat and Republican, who remain reelected year after year largely because they have played the game and have won expenditures for manufacturers in their districts. In Chapter VII, he even relates:

> The one weapon that you don't need in the fight against terrorists is a new submarine with a 2.5 billion dollar price tag that was designed to defeat Soviet subs in a battle to control the deep seas. The Soviets are gone, and what remains of their sub fleet in Russian hands is poorly maintained and rarely allowed to submerge for long journeys. So clearly, the fifty-two attack submarines kept by the United States at peak performance are without a worthy adversary, and one is not about to be launched by stateless terrorists like Al Qaeda.[2]

---

1. Scheer, *The Pornography of Power,* 33–34
2. Scheer, *The Pornography of Power,* 36–37

Mr. Scher's book should be read by every American who really wants to know who or what they are voting for and paying for. Another book that I hope the reader will examine is entitled "Addicted to War" by Joel Andreas. The book is called an "illustrated" book because the speakers are actually drawn characters. However, the book and its contents are anything but comical. As explained earlier, I am hopeful that my book is "simple" and "little" because it is written for those of us who are busy, hard- working people who need authors that can share their thoughts with them without burdening them with long drawn-out theoretical writing after working all day. I am recommending Mr. Andreas' book for the same reason. It, too, is a "simple" and "little" book, but it is filled with facts and figures, the kind of facts and figures we should all want to have before us. In fact, "Addicted to War" not only traces the history of our military industrial system, but even names the corporations whose villainous tentacles are robbing us of the very democracy they are pretending to protect and serve. They are, or already have, *become* government.

First, let's imagine we are in a school room or a church hall, or even our church itself. We all know the "Pledge of Allegiance", right? OK. Let us first recite the Pledge of Allegiance.

> I pledge allegiance to the flag of the United States of America, and to the Republic for which it stands, one nation, under God, indivisible, with liberty, and justice, for all.

Now, we are going to do something that will have a different effect on different kinds of people. Some of us will think it is silly, and, some of us might feel a little unsettled, or even threatened. Repeat (to yourself) after me:

> I pledge allegiance. . .to the flag, of the Military Industrial Complex, and to the Republic which it now owns, one nation, Under God, indivisible, with liberty and justice, for all.

It sounds a little bit silly for some, and might even elicit some anger from others. But this "simple little book" was written not to entertain, but to provoke some Catholics into thinking a little bit harder not only about their faith, but about what many of us might actually be perpetuating.

Finally, let's go back to a very prophetic speech given by President Dwight D. Eisenhower; his "farewell address" to the nation in nineteen fifty-nine. President Eisenhower said:

> Until the latest of our world conflicts, The United States had no armaments industry. American makers of plowshares could, with time and as required, make swords as well. But now we can longer risk emergency improvisation of national defense. We have been compelled to create a permanent armaments industry of vast proportions. Added to this, three and a half million men and women are directly engaged in the defense establishment. We annually spend on military security more than the net income of all United States corporations.

Notice the "permanent" nature of the military industrial establishment by the time this speech was written.

President Eisenhower went on to say:

> In the councils of government, we must guard against the acquisition of unwarranted influence, whether sought or unsought, by the military-industrial complex. The potential for the disastrous rise of misplaced power exists and willpersist. . . We must never let the weight of this combination endanger our liberty or democratic processes. We should take nothing for granted. Only an alert and knowledgeable citizenry can compel the proper use of the huge industrial and military machinery of defense with our peaceful methods and goals, so that security and liberty may prosper together.

As an aside, the story is told that President Eisenhower originally planned to address the involvement of legislators in his speech, by describing the "military industrial congressional complex." His advisors asked him to remove the references to congressional legislators so that the American people would not become disillusioned with their government.

A careful reading of President Eisenhower's speech can only yield to us two conclusions:

1. President Eisenhower saw the military-industrial complex coming, and,

2. the military industrial complex saw us coming.

Lastly, there is a logic among American Catholics that escapes me. I am noticing that fewer and fewer of us read. We are especially content to listen to one or two abrupt statements we should call "one-liners" usually uttered by television journalists. We invariably tune in to television channels that we know beforehand will reinforce our biases, and seemingly never admit that we insist on settling for the simplest explanation for world events that are placed before us. We fetishize the military and invariably insist that so-and-so is away "protecting our freedoms." I am led to the question: how can the military industrial complex protect freedoms that we have already relinquished?

5

Political . . . Idolatry???

(POWER OR FORCE . . . WE'RE GETTING WARM!)

IT IS NOT TOO far-fetched to regard nationalism as idolatry once the above-referenced satanic carnage is seen. Like every serious thinking religious community, an adult critical reading of the scriptures gives us the needed insight. As written earlier, Jesus gives us a distinct picture of Satan in John's Gospel when He calls Satan ". . . a liar and. . .a murderer from the beginning." Once an adult reading of the scriptures is accepted, there is no turning back. The "lie" of nationalism (more specifically, the "lie" of its holiness) and the consequent "murder" by and for the so-called nation is before our eyes if we can find the intelligence and the courage to look. "Modern" because in the nuclear age, the once-upon a time "revered" nation state can no longer be part of our here and now.

It is clear that ". . .the doctrine that national interests. . .are more important than international interests. . ." (remember that we consulted the dictionary) precludes anyone steeped in nationalism from being able to claim to harbor a truly Catholic worldview. (consistent with Fr. de Chardin). The world is redeemed, not one's so-called "country." Nationalism stands directly in the path of a world-wide faith. (Fr. Teilhard de Chardin) An otherwise Catholic parish engulfed by nationalism has to face the fact that their Catholicism has at best been deeply eroded.

Other voices are raised when the fear of idolatrous nationalism is felt. Modernly, a good place to look for leadership on this issue is Dietrich Bonhoeffer, a German pastor and martyr. Before being executed by the Nazis, Bonhoeffer, a member of the German resistance, taught us of the idolatrous nature of nationalism. But before he could do that, he had to become the kind of man that would never yield to the ". . .passions. . ." referenced by Dr. Schlabach in his June 2017 article in Commonweal. In the biography "Bonhoeffer: Pastor, Martyr, Prophet, Spy" he is described by the author, Eric Metaxas in the following manner:

> He had been reared to guard against parochialism and to assiduously avoid relying on feelings or anything unsupported by reasoning. During his lifetime, Bonhoeffer brought this critical and scientific attitude to all questions of faith and theology.[1]

This is to say that one of the most prominent ethicists of the twentieth century never allowed the emotionality of nationalism to divert his attention from Christ. Even in the face of martyrdom at the hands of Hitler, he would never permit in his own soul the mixing of Christianity with the nation state. Once a Catholic allows himself or herself to come to regard their nation state as being in any way comparable to God or sacralized, like any addiction, it, as a process, becomes very difficult to reverse. That is why Bonhoeffer said:

> If you board the wrong train, it is no use running along the corridor in the opposite direction.[2]

There are voices of warning today.

This is obviously not just a Catholic problem. In an article dated January 11, 2013, Craig M. Watts published the following

1. Metaxas, *Boenhoffer: Pastor, Martyr, Prophet, Spy*, 54
2. Metaxas, *Boenhoffer: Pastor, Martyr, Prophet, Spy*, 187

story in "Red Letter Christians" entitled "Taking the Words of Jesus Seriously: Daring to Call It Idolatry: Nationalism in Worship." He tells of a "bright young couple" who began to attend the church he served. The young man, a Baptist minister from an Eastern European country, eventually related that he could no longer worship at the church that had sponsored his wife earlier as a missionary, because he stated that "worship there is too much about American patriotism than real worship." Rev. Craig's article went straight to the heart of the matter by saying:

> What we do in worship speaks of who God is and who we are as the sort of people who are capable of following no other god but the God of Israel who was disclosed most fully in Jesus Christ. When acts celebrating America are treated as aspects of worshiping and serving God, Christian identity, the nature of the church and the character of God are misrepresented. All this negatively impacts discipleship and undermines Christian unity in a divided world, thereby hindering church in its ministry of reconciliation.

It is nationalism of the type described above that ". . . hinders. . ." the church's ". . .ministry of reconciliation. . ." The inescapable reality that there is only one redeemed world is a fact not allowable in the mindset of nationalism.

6

Fascism

WHERE THERE WAS SMOKE, NOW FIRE IS BREAKING OUT

THERE WAS A TIME when I thought I had finished this book. But then the ultimate catastrophe which can accompany hyper-nationalism actually began to rear its ugly head. Political events which occurred very recently led to the risk of our "morphing" from hyper-nationalism to its dark, ugly progeny, fascism. Our vulnerability to fascism might come largely through our tendency to try to angrily oversimplify the world by grasping at simple solutions to complex problems; problems that our faith should allow us to weather.

The appeal of authoritarian government is now intense among roughly half of the Catholic population in the United States. As much as our Catholic faith should distinguish us from the secular world around us, it is not doing so. If we are honest, we can say that we have recently seen an attempt at overriding a presidential election by force. Not-so-subtle warnings remain. We continue to experience tangible evidence of the appeal of fascism among us.

Here it should be noted that the mythical picture of dictatorial fascism as an abrupt and instantaneous seizure of power is no longer reliable. Modernly, that is not how democracies die. In "How Democracies Die" Steven Levitsky and Daniel Ziblatt teach us that the modern "death" of a democracy such as ours occurs when a demagogue is lawfully elected. The characteristic promise of simple solutions to complex problems typically carries the demagogue to power. Then the gradual erosion of the democracy begins.

A brief reference to St. Paul is helpful here. One might equate the promise of simple solutions to complex problems as a kind of illusory diamond. Where Paul warns us that ". . .the wages of sin are death. . ." we would do well to imagine the following picture.

An anxious man or woman unknowingly walks past a pool of quicksand. He or she lives in the mistaken belief that all of their seemingly complex problems will be simplified by wealth. As luck would have it, our shiny but illusory diamond, to represent the temptation to sin, is perched on a rock in the middle of the quicksand. The ". . .wages of sin. . ." become death. A sudden mindless lunge toward the diamond permanently ends the "simple solutions to complex problems." The quicksand quickly claims the passerby in the mistaken belief that fascism will solve the problems.

But we are called to carry our seemingly complex problems to our Catholic faith. To answer the basic question "what is fascism" we must examine fascism and determine what it really means and more importantly what it will really do to our lives. But in doing that we must understand that we only "scratch the surface" of the issue by limiting ourselves to the socio/political understanding of fascism. Dictionary definitions and historical examples can only take us so far. We must attempt to understand fascism when compared to our Catholic faith. Further, most if not all definitions of fascism seem to be descriptive of fascism only as a political phenomenon and avoid its moral implications.

Wikipedia defines fascism as ". . .a form of authoritarian ultranationalism characterized by dictatorial power, forcible suppression of opposition, and strong regimentation of society and of the economy, often racist, etc." But for our purposes as Catholics, we must look beyond definitions of fascism that paint fascism simply as a socio/political phenomenon.

Historically we know of the moral degradation that occurs in the lives of people who succumb to fascism. We know of the Holocaust and fascism's moral degradation of the human soul through the idolatrous "de facto worship" (ultranationalism) of the nation state and its demagogues. Fascism's brutal history has left permanent scars on the human community. When we look much deeper, beyond the dictionary's definition of fascism and into the moral aspects of fascism, we find its proponents taking the human community deep into the realm of pure evil; evil such as the Holocaust and so-called "all out" warfare" in which the people of entire nations are enticed to become immeasurably violent.

And fascism in the nuclear age seems even more threatening in that entire populations of priceless human beings could be eradicated in hours through the evil machinations or even the bungling footsteps of a single incompetent demagogue. To relate these concerns to our Catholic faith we must be willing to go much deeper into the realm of "evil." We must not settle for political definitions of fascism. And spiritually and prayerfully, in order to look at evil, we must be willing go into the "other side" of the human experience. We must talk about idolatry and sin.

But will thoughtful Catholics pick up the ball? There are now many Catholic organizations responsibly addressing the issue of fascism. There are peace and Justice workers in Pax Christi and those Catholic journalists who write and literally live the peace movement. They have a keen understanding of fascism and its implications. Then there are all of the hundreds of people who work in and through the dozens of Catholic Worker houses in the United States. They see fascism's resultant poverty which follows our obsession with military spending. They are equally aware of the danger we are in. All are filled with a vibrant religious faith. But if asked, they would tell us that throughout all of their social justice work, they know that today, they are working to address fascism.

In this life we probably cannot thoroughly understand evil per se, but we cannot fail to attempt to discuss it in the context of fascism. That means that we must go one step farther (into the other side) in our efforts at understanding fascism. One author, Mark Colville of the Kings Bay plowshares Seven wrote:

> Fascism, in its essence, is not a political system or a form of government. It is a moral disorder in which masses of people through a pervasive combination of trauma and propaganda succumb to a progressive demonization by the Principalities and Powers of most or all of the human values that enable us to coexist in peace.

Perhaps now is the time to inch closer to a real definition of fascism. It is time to talk about the "de facto worship" of the nation state in the form of idolatry.

Many Catholics may find it hard to talk about sin in the context of fascism for two reasons. First, as discussed, we have been accustomed to seeing fascism strictly as a political phenomenon and not in any way related to our sense of morality. When we talk about sin, we usually mean some form of serious personal misconduct entirely unrelated to any political issue. For example, there are the sexual encounters that are not only sinful but personally destructive. Then there are ethical breaches such as theft and fraud. But these kinds of sin do not disrupt or destroy whole communities, certainly not at a national level. But, because we have all but stopped using the word "idolatry" we have failed to see the "de facto worship" of the nation state, fascism, for what it really is.

Perhaps it was well said by father Gregory Baum, a German born scholar turned Canadian priest when he said:

> Personal sin is freely chosen. Social sin is collective blindness. There is sin as deed and sin as illness."

FASCISM REARS ITS UGLY HEAD

We seemingly have one more feature of fascism that must be discussed; the demagogue, the final piece of our working definition of our seemingly elusive puzzle. But what exactly is a demagogue? let us once again consult our dictionary where we find ". . . a person, especially a political leader, who wins support by exciting people's emotions rather than giving them reasons. . ."

We have begun to learn not only what fascism consists of but where it will take us. If one prefers a biblical approach, we have only to visit the ancient story of the Golden Calf. In Mose's absence the Israelites panicked and erected a golden calf, seemingly what one author called "a desperately formed pretension of leadership" or perhaps an idol, or a demagogue if you will. We are not told exactly what punishment was brought down upon the Israelites. However, the important lesson to be learned in the area of Judeo-Christian teaching seems to be "create an extra god, and your community will suffer the consequences."

Even if an American expression of fascism never reached outside our shores, which in today's interconnected world seems impossible, demagogues are not in the habit of competently managing societies. And no one for that matter anticipates the demagogue's accepting responsibility for the suffering that follows in his wake. And as always is the case God's poor will suffer the most.

Many Catholics today raise the objection that the church should "remain out of politics" and that the church should simply "preach the Catholic faith" and avoid any political issues. The present-day objection to some of the church's Bishops and clerics speaking out on political issues is not rooted in factual, responsible and even historical realities. As recently as World War II, when fascism became the scourge of much of Europe, the church was very vocal in its condemnation of fascism and of those who had succumbed to "the lure of authoritarianism."

On June 29, 1931, Pope Pius XI published an encyclical entitled "Non Abiammo Bisogno" (Italian for "We do not need") in which he condemned Italian fascism's "pagan worship of the state" (using the word "state-ology" to mean literally the de facto worship of the state). There can be no question where fascism ultimately took Europe. Pope Pius went straight to the heart of the matter in defining fascism (state-ology) as a form of idolatry. We reap what we sew.

To compare our present-day endangerment to those of Europe's some 90 years ago would undoubtedly tempt us to regard their phenomenal fascism as being irrelevant to our lives. That would be a mistake. The Catholic population of 1938 Germany was undergoing the same suffering as was the rest of the German population. Poverty and unemployment were rampant. People were literally starving, largely as a result of the hardships imposed by the allies of World War I. Inflation climbed to an immeasurable rate and I can recall seeing photographs of German women burning worthless currency in wood burning stoves to heat the little food they had. We Americans do not have the "German excuse" today. For the most part usually the poorest among us can be reasonably sure of having food to eat and a roof over their heads, and most of our poorest have at least marginal health care.

Ducking The Issue

In reply to our challenge, there can be no question that there is a typical "Diocesan" homily with the following attributes. There is a reference to Jesus, and His love and the Father's love for us. There is a direct reference to the reality of the Eucharist and the sacraments. There are myriad references to all of the expressions of piety and righteousness that are expected to appear in our lives. But in the last analysis, there is never any hint or for that matter any implied reference to our penchant for nationalism.

There is seldom or never even a subtle warning that excessive nationalism under the guise of "patriotism" can amount to a form of worship; the idolatrous "de facto worship" of the nation state.

The same concern arises when one contemplates the "de facto worship" of our demagogues. This in turn gives way to the American Parish business model. There is never any reference to "politics" because some parishioners may be "offended" if they take the statement as a criticism of their political party or any government policy which they support. But it seems, that the priest is however always permitted to encourage "national loyalty" or so called "patriotism" but it must be devoid of any applied or limiting moral standard. Strict uncritical adulation of "the flag" alone is permitted. But that is not the point. The American parish business model will not allow any priest or Pastor to warn, even implicitly, of the dangers of national or partisan loyalty so extreme that the nation state to which a parishioner "pledges his or her allegiance" can and does become a form of worship. This is not theoretical. I have met them.

We are not suffering from what I would call the German model of fascism. Although we are not suffering the privations similar to the privations of the German Catholics during the 1930s, something else is happening to us here in the United States that we do not yet understand. The unmistakable signs of fascism loom, and even those of us who are succumbing to it cannot for the most part explain themselves or their "de facto worship" of a nation-state through a demagogue.

Almost half of the Catholics in the United States, like half of the American population, have been seduced by authoritarianism. We are unknowingly growing tired of the democracy about which we have boasted all of our lives. What choices are we about to make?

I realize that there exists within this writing and implied dichotomy in which two objects of worship or idolatrous veneration are proposed. One is overtly identified, the nation state itself as a "de facto" object of worship. The other implied object of worship is the demagogue himself. and at this point it should be said that one demagogue can easily be replaced by another.

Demagoguery is explained and described by two cognitive research psychologists named David Dunning and Justin Kruger of Cornell University. The Dunning-Kruger effect in psychology is a cognitive bias whereby people with limited knowledge or competence in a given intellectual or social domain greatly overestimate their own knowledge or competence in the domain relative to objective criteria. According to the researchers for whom it is named, the Dunning- Kruger effect is explained by the fact that the metacognitive ability to recognize deficiencies in one's own knowledge requires that one possess at least a minimum level of the same kind of knowledge or competence which those who exhibit the effect have not attained. Because they are unaware of their deficiencies, such people generally assume that they are not deficient. The Dunning- Kruger effect is described as:

> . . . a type of cognitive bias where people with little expertise or ability assume they have Superior expertise or ability. This overestimation occurs as a result of the fact that they don't have enough knowledge to know they don't have enough knowledge . . . unskilled and unaware of it; how difficulties in recognizing one's own incompetence leads to one's inflated self-assessment.[1]

A dilemma is presented to us. The Dilemma consists of the fact that it has been argued that both the demagogue and the nation state are presented to us as objects of de facto worship. In dangerous situations such as our current one either one can be. The question becomes does the presence of demagoguery within the ranks of some American Catholics serve as our portal into fascism, or does extreme nationalism alone create the risk?

It would appear that excessive nationalism, the "de facto worship" of the nation state is the most culpable and dangerous of the two "objects of worship." That is because in alluding to the Kruger-Dunning effect, we learned that the demagogue contains within himself the seeds of his own social and political destruction. His flamboyant narcissism will be his own undoing. But the nation state is a relatively permanent fixture in the world. It is the nation state that outlasts all of the other social entities that often demand our unfaltering allegiance. As a pseudo-legal institution, the nation state alone sometimes demands that we relinquish our capacity and our willingness to engage in critical thinking. It is the nation state that requires us to kill. As a behaviorist might say, "that is what a god is, because that is what a god does."

---

1. Kruger and Dunning. *The Journal of Psychology and Personality,* Vol. 82 p.

7

Jesus or the Sword?

A CHOICE IS DEMANDED OF US

Since The Nuclear Age began in 1945, we have been confronted
with the demand that a choice be made; a choice between war as a
fact of life, or war as being avoidable. But the fact of the catastrophic nature of war in the nuclear age is now being forced upon us. Up
until the modern age, war, as painful and destructive as it has always been, has been survivable. Now war in the nuclear age brings
us the prospect of the complete destruction of human civilization
as we know it. There are still those Americans who walk about
speaking of war in terms of tanks and artillery; about *bombing* cities. Once and for all, we are required to learn; in a modern-day
nuclear war, cities will not be *bombed*; cities, and every living soul
within them, will be *melted*. Those of us who cannot imagine that,
share in the responsibility for the endangerment brought about by
the nuclear arms race. And we must also accept the fact that even
in the case of a so-called conventional war erupting, the danger of
escalation into a nuclear exchange is always present.

The Catholic Church in its world-wide reach through the
Vatican first addressed the threat of nuclear war through the

Second Vatican Council, or Vatican II between October of 1962 and December of 1965. The Council opened with its evaluation of modern warfare by teaching that "the whole human race faces a moment of supreme crisis in its advance toward maturity." More recently, on the crisis before us in the form of the nuclear arms race, the American National Conference of Catholic Bishops subsequently reached out to you and I in May of 1983. The topic of nuclear war is now unavoidable in the context of an "Americanized Gospel." That is because it is not only the nation state that can bring about a nuclear confrontation, we may do so through our "Americanized Gospel" ourselves by allowing nationalism to be preached in our churches and through the bungling of an inept demagogue. We are learning that the nation state may wield enough power over our minds and our lives to bring about nuclear war. We Catholics are not immune from the curse of "holy nationalism."

For our purposes, a conversation about the nuclear arms race should in fact follow our earlier conversation about fascism. That is because upon gaining an awareness about the nature of fascism and its demagoguery we can now endeavor to pair that awareness with an awareness of the nature of the weaponry that, upon our succumbing to fascism, would fall into the hands of fascism's proponents; fascism's demagogues.

In the event that some Catholic readers might continue to feel that the Church either does not or should not publicly address political issues, we need only to go to the United States Catholic bishops' outcry of May 3, 1983. That is the date upon which our National Conference of Catholic Bishops published "THE CHALLENGE OF PEACE; God's Promise and Our Response."

After that very fateful date (and "fateful" is the right word), the Catholic laity was no longer free to "look the other way" with impunity on the topic of the nuclear arms race. As our current chapter's title alerts us, "a decision is required" on the question of "Jesus or The Sword?" In the document cited above, we ignore this issue at our own peril in two different ways. First, we fail in our calling to promote peace by funding a nuclear stockpile unparalleled in human history, thereby endangering every human life on earth. Secondly, and of equal importance, we fail by allowing our resources to be deterred away from the poor into the coffers of arms manufacturers.

Although some of our readers might still feel somehow "annoyed" at the Church's speaking out on so-called "political issues," the Church is meeting Her obligation to alert us to the spiritual and temporal folly inherent in the nuclear arms race. The National Conference of Catholic Bishops has worked to meet their obligation to us. That is why the document is called "A Pastoral Letter." Our Catholic bishops themselves assert their teaching responsibility into the realm of our so-called "political life." Our so-called "political lives" are not beyond the reach of our Savior or His Church. The Risen Christ, through this document, sends His shepherds into our midst; into our so-called "political lives."

The Conference's document is not a short one by any standard. However, a number of points stand out. The document begins by affirming that the source of the document is The Second Vatican Council, or "Vatican Two."

> The Second Vatican Council opened its evaluation of modern warfare with the statement 'the whole human race faces a moment of supreme crisis in its advance towards maturity.' We agree with the Council's assessment: the crisis of the moment is embodied in the threat which nuclear weapons pose for the world and much that we hold dear in the world."

Later in the document the bishops state:

> The arms race is one of the greatest curses on the human race. It is to be condemned as a danger, an act of aggression against the poor.

Here something even more interesting is repeated. The bishops not only condemn nuclear weapons, but we are reminded that whenever we apply our resources to the arms race, we take those same resources away from the poor. I am reminded of the John Denver song entitled "What Are We Making Weapons For?" The lyrics go on to say ". . .we take it away from the mouths of our babies. We take it away from the hands of the poor. Tell me what are we making weapons for?"

Perhaps for that reason, in another paragraph, the bishops go so far as to say that the nuclear arms race has "cosmic dimensions."

In the event one is tempted to object that the nuclear arms race ". . .isn't [addressed] in the Bible. . ." (one hears that objection regarding many issues), the Conference addresses this objection by stating:

> Even a brief examination of war and peace in the scrip-
> tures makes it clear that they do not provide us with de-
> tailed answers to the specifics of the questions which we
> face today. They do not speak specifically of nuclear war
> or nuclear weapons, for these were beyond the imagina-
> tion of the communities in which the scriptures were
> formed."

Lastly, there is a section withing the document labeled "The New Moment." Therein, the Conference tells us:

> At the center of the new evaluation of the nuclear arms
> race is a recognition of two elements; the destructive
> potential of nuclear weapons, and the stringent choices
> which the nuclear age poses for both politics and morals.

Something else "New" may have happened here. The Church has always conserved or guarded documents and writings that have been handed down by the saints of the earlier Church. As dis-cussed earlier, Saint Augustine of Hippo has given us the "Just War Theory," and Saint Thomas Acquinas has refined it to some extent. Does this "New Moment" spoken of within Today's Conference approach or implicitly state the realization that irrespective of the theoretical criteria of the past, the so-called Just War Theory *has now become obsolete*?

The following paragraphs will hopefully serve to encourage today's working Catholics that there are scores of responsible, prayerful, informed and energized Catholics who are literally putting their bodies on the line in an effort to push back against the nuclear arms race. In other words, those Catholic men and women, lay and religious, young and old standing for "peace" and a sane world are not "crackpots." They are making their sacrifices for you and I.

DOROTHY DAY

It is almost impossible to address the Church's responsibility to confront the American Catholic Church's role in the nuclear arms race without acknowledging Dorothy Day. As a convert to Catholicism, she was an extremely persistent and vocal activist. Some would argue that her greatest lifelong achievement would be the founding of The Catholic Worker in total service to the poor in 1933, along with her friend Peter Maurin. Although her birth preceded Vatican II and The American Catholic Bishops' Conference by decades, as well as the nuclear age, throughout her adult life she was a very active member of the Church as she demonstrated publicly against poverty, racism, and militarism. For our purposes, she became a powerful Catholic voice against the nuclear arms race upon its arrival into our history. And again, in her outspoken complaint as to how the arms race took resources away from the poor, we hear our friend, John Denver, in his song:

> What Are We Making Weapons For?" Why keep on feeding the war machine? We take it away from the mouths of our babies; we take it away from the hands of the poor.

THOMAS MERTON

The reader will surely have heard of Thomas Merton the spiritual mentor. His writings and poetry have given all Americans a wealth of insights into the spiritual life and God's own willingness to enter into our own prayer lives.

Thomas Merton was born in France and led a reasonably "restless" life as a young man. A dramatic set of tragic events befell him in his early life that I have always suspected somehow served as the underpinnings of the spiritual transformation he obviously underwent.

While at Cambridge he fathered a child who he never met. Merton's dowry apparently served to meet his financial responsibilities to both the mother and the child, but by most reports both were killed in the London blitz of World War II.

So much for the assumption that monks and spiritual writers do not "feel" or "know about" the world.

Merton found his way to the United States and at the age of twenty-eight he entered the Trappist community at Gethsemane, Kentucky. Throughout his life he wrote volumes about the spiritual life and prayer. It might be the case that he is best known for his writings about the so-called "true self" as opposed to the so-called "false self." According to Merton, the "false self" is a personal identity that is either assigned to us by the world around us or is intentionally adopted by one who "bought into" one or more of the world's "labels." The "true self" however is of course the "hidden" self that God would have us find through the depths of prayer. It is this "true self" that should be the object of our personal "journey."

Here it should be suggested that the Catholic community as a community should be embarking on the same "journey" to find the "true collective self," and the dawn of the nuclear age is evidently the point in history at which this "journey" must be undertaken. For that reason, Merton did not confine himself to so-called "God and Me" spirituality. Being very informed and insightful in terms of the state of the world, he addressed, among other forms of violence, the ultimate form of violence today; the nuclear arms race and the possibility of nuclear war.

Gregory Hillis wrote a wonderfully helpful piece about Thomas Merton in the April 8, 2022 issue of America entitled "Thomas Merton Can Still Teach Us a Lot About Nuclear War."

In Mr. Hillis' article he reports to us about how Thomas Merton stood publicly against the nuclear arms race, and by extension, the risk of nuclear war.

The article begins by acknowledging that the nuclear issue has not been in the forefront of our discussions as American

Catholics, but the risk is now reappearing in light of the Russian invasion of Ukraine and the growing tension between China and Taiwan. Mr. Hillis then invites us to again "return to Merton's writings on nuclear weapons and the Christian responsibility to advocate for peace in the nuclear age."

In general, our book tries to address the current state in which the American Church finds herself in terms of the leadership she should be reflecting to American Catholics on the nuclear issue.

Mr. Hillis writes:

> Compelled by a strong sense of the dignity of all human life, Merton reacted with incredulity not only to the possibility that humanity could doom itself to annihilation through nuclear war, but that American Catholics-including some priests and bishops supported America's use of its nuclear arsenal in a first strike against Russia.

We are asked to recall that we found that the American Conference of Catholic Bishops seemed to at least implicitly conclude that the so-called "Just War Theory" had become obsolete. Mr. Hillis writes:

> However, he [Merton] came to the conclusion that the just war tradition no longer had relevance given the destructive capabilities of contemporary weaponry, especially nuclear weaponry.

Then Merton himself is quoted:

> I am not a pure pacifist in theory though today in practice I don't see how one can be anything else, since limited wars, (however 'just') present an almost certain danger of nuclear war on an all-out scale.

Mr. Hillis finishes his article by expressing his optimism that the American Church is now beginning to move away from the Just War Theory, even if we are doing so in a slow cautious manner. He also makes reference to the fact that more than one recent Pope has expressed their concerns on the nuclear issue, urging us to act more responsibly. Lastly, Mr. Hillis makes it clear that

Thomas Merton would unquestionably oppose any use of any nuclear weapons under any circumstances.

DANIEL BERRIGAN

It would be impossible to address the American Catholic Church's response to the nuclear arms race without discussing Daniel Berrigan. I have obtained permission from the author of an article about Thomas Merton from which I will take excerpts. The article written by a good friend, Fr. John Dear. The article appeared on the website of Fr. Daniel Berrigan, and can be found in its entire form at https://danielberrigan.org/biography/. The reader is invited to read the entire article.

I only had the privilege of meeting Daniel Berrigan on one occasion at a demonstration in Concord, California years ago. He was a Jesuit priest and is described as having been an anti-war activist and a Christian pacifist who spoke out against poverty, racism, and for our purposes, permanentized warfare, especially through the nuclear arms race. It is again urged that ours is a form of permanentized warfare in that the military industrial complex has now become fundamental to our national economy.

Father Berrigan was born on May 9, 1921 and entered the Jesuit Society as a young man in 1939. He was ordained to the priesthood on June 19, 1952. He is described as being "devoted to the Catholic Church throughout his youth." During a visit to Paris, he met several Jesuits who were very critical of the social and political conditions in Indochina. It is reported that from these meetings came the founding of the Catholic Peace Fellowship by both himself and his fellow priest and brother Father Phillip Berrigan, also S.J.

Throughout the following years, he taught at several universities. Apparently, given his "awakening" in Paris regarding the issue of the Vietnam war, his public activism began. But in conjunction with the Vietnam war's issues, there immediately followed the next natural step. That was to speak out publicly against the nuclear arms race and the permanent nature of arms production, to include nuclear weapons.

One early public act of resistance against nuclear weapons occurred on May 17, 1968 at the offices of the draft board in Cantonsville, Maryland. There, Father Berrigan and eight other activists, to include his brother Phillip, used homemade napalm to destroy some 358 draft files in opposition to militarism.

As we learned earlier, many Catholics are critical of the Church's apparent inability to speak out against a permanentized military industrial complex. After the incident at Cantonsville, the "Cantonsville Nine" issued a statement expressing their disappointment with the Church in that regard.

> We confront the Roman Catholic Church, other Christian bodies, and the synagogues of America with their silence and cowardice in the face of our country's crimes. We are convinced that the religious bureaucracy in is racist, is an accomplice in this war, and is hostile to the poor.

(Throughout this writing, as a generalization, a distinction has often been made between "comfortable suburban parishes" and those parishes who are confronted with the poor daily, and respond to their needs with temporal assistance. It is hoped that these distinctions are made fairly. I have watched a number of Saint Vincent De Paul chapters flourish, along with other organizations, and, as a Catholic, I am proud of them).

Daniel Berrigan was arrested and sentenced to three years in prison. Although he went into hiding, the Federal Bureau of Investigation eventually apprehended him. He was released in 1972.

By 1980, it was all about the nuclear arms race. Daniel Berrigan and his brother Phillip, along with six others, formed the "Ploughshares" movement. The movement's name is rooted in Isaiah's biblical mandate to "beat one's sword into a plowshare." The "Plowshares Eight" then trespassed onto the General Electric nuclear facility in King of Prussia, Pennsylvania and poured blood onto documents and files. They then were arrested with numerous felonies and underwent years of legal proceeding before being ultimately paroled

MORE PLOWSHARES

The Kings Bay Plowshares 7

The Kings Bay Plowshares are a group of seven Catholics peace activists who broke into the Kings Bay Naval Submarine base and carried out a symbolic act of protest against nuclear weapons. The name and the action and the wider anti-nuclear Plowshares movement again comes from the prophet Isaiah's command to "beat swords into plowshares."

Kings Bay Naval Base was the home port to a submarine squadron with at least five "Ohio Class" ballistic missile submarines, each of which was said to be capable of carrying twenty four Trident II missiles with nuclear weapons.

The Kings Bay Plowshares Seven took action on April 4, 2018, after considerable prayer and discernment. They cut through a security fence and entered the base unlawfully. They are said to have been "singing and praying" during the trespass. Their banner, even today, reads: "The Ultimate Logic of Trident: Omnicide," and their photograph as a group is visible in many publications. They poured their own blood on an official seal of the base. They damaged a display of a missel with a hammer as one of them read Pope Francis' denouncement of nuclear weapons.

They were subsequently tried as a group in a Federal District Court in Georgia. Their logical explanation to the jury was a denial of any criminal intent, but they wanted to testify by entering the so-called "necessity defense" in that they were making an effort to prevent the crime of nuclear war. Here it should be mentioned that the "necessity defense" is frequently used in criminal trials of peace activists, but the Federal District Court in the trial of the Seven disallowed it. Further, for some inexplicable reason, they were not permitted to enter into testimony any reference to their religious motivations.

In October of 2019, a Federal Grand jury found the Seven guilty. The names of the Seven are:

Carmen Trotta

Patrick O'Neill

Elizabeth McAllister

Steve Kelly

Martha Hennessy, the granddaughter of Dorothy Day.

Clare Grady

Mark Colville, who we quoted in our chapter on fascism.

In an effort to provide a brief background on each of the Kings Bay Plowshares Seven, we will use excerpts from some of their addresses to the court during their sentencing hearings.

Mark Colville's post sentencing statement read in part:

> My neighborhood , my family and I have a right to live without a nuclear gun on hair trigger alert held perpetually to our heads. That right is ours, both by birth and by law. It is neither granted by courts nor denied by them, but this court's refusal to defend that right- or even to recognize it- has now, with no fewer than 28 convictions against me and my companions, placed it firmly in a posture of criminality. On this, the world agrees, as the international consensus prohibiting the building and law, by ratified treaty, on January 21st of this year. This court was given a responsibility to all of those neighborhoods and to me. It was a charge that the times demanded and still demand; an obligation that emanates directly from the conscience of the human community, and which the court ultimately refused to accept. That law to be applied beyond the fence at Kings Bay; that fence behind which this government, in its lawlessness, has hidden lawlessness, has first strike weapons with enough firepower to kill 6 billion people; a fence that I and my loved ones, with much fear and trembling, freely answered the call of faith , the call of conscience, and the call of generations yet unborn to breach.

It is to be noted that Mark Colville, in addressing the court, referenced both the illegality of the court's sentencing and, under

national law, the illegality of the stockpiled nuclear weapons themselves. But we also know that Mr. Colville also harbors a deep faith,
having earlier defined fascism as a "moral disorder."

Martha Hennessey sentencing statement referencing her
deep religious faith stated:

> I am attempting to transform the fundamental values of
> public life. I am willing to suffer for the common good,
> and for our sin of not loving our brothers, a condition
> that leads to war. War stems from our unwillingness to
> love one another as Christ has loved us. This is what the
> Bomb means to me.

As is the case with Mark Colville and all of the Kings Bay
Plowshares Seven, their arguments referencing the illegality of
"the Bomb" are paired with their deep religious faith. The quotations from Mark Colville and Martha Hennessey are basically consistent with the remaining Five. All of their sentencing quotations
may be found on line under the Google heading of "The Kingsbay
Plowshares Seven."

Something very imported must be stated and restated here.
To speak out or to in any way react to any social evil, whether it is
poverty, racism, or the nuclear arms race, two things must be done.

First, there must be a **public action**. It is pointless to enter a
closet and whisper to ones' self about any social evil, although that
might be the proper setting for prayer. The systems that maintain
that evil must be confronted, even if they are populated by either
laymen, priests, or bishops.

Second, it must be understood that more often than not, **a
price must be paid** by any so-called "activist." If ones' outcry does
not at least bring about the scorn of the systems that maintain the
social evil, one has not "acted." If ones' outcry does not in any way
challenge the social order that maintains the social evil, one has
not "acted."

Something more must be noted. All of the people we heard of
in this chapter, from Dorothy Day to Thomas Merton, to the Kings
Bay Plowshares Seven were at one earlier point in time so-called
"ordinary" Catholics like you and I. They attended Mass, they went

to confession, they read about their faith, and most importantly, they maintained a "serious" prayer life. But at some point in time, something "unordinary" happened to them. Without knowing exactly how any spiritual "upheaval" occurs in any person, I would argue that a powerful and very basic realization was given to them. Above and beyond their understand of militarism and "the bomb", they were confronted by the Holy Spirit with the fact that they are God's children, and God's children alone. They never did and never will look to the nation state for a personal identity. The same "miracle" or "realization" is available to anyone that can find the intelligence and the courage to act on the impulse. That is the crux of the book we are reading, and that is how we will finish our book in the last chapters.

8

Is There a Catholic Style?

Is THERE A UNIQUELY Catholic way to make the mistake of political idolatry? There might be. Admittedly, it is rarely the case that a parish priest will stand up in the pulpit and give a homily overtly praising and blessing and extolling the virtues of the parish's "country", although I have seen it done. But it is typically the case that when members of the parish do make it clear that their "flag" is entitled to a reverence similar to the reverence due to God, the local "clergy" look the other way. Often the comfortable suburban parish maintains this "American Catholic Style" by making the mistake of sacralizing its "country" or its "nation" like the woman in our televangelist's event we saw earlier, but it is done largely through silence.

I again describe a conversation I had with a parish priest in a market in which I complained that there was too much nationalism in my parish. I even suggested that it was espoused by too many parishioners, and even "preached" in a subtle manner. The priest-friend replied that it was not done "from the pulpit." But being a parish priest in a comfortable, suburban parish, he had "customers" to please. For that reason, his reply is easily translated:

"yes, we do have a great deal of 'flag worship' in our parish, in spite of the fact that there is only one Jesus. However, that is how the 'customers' feel and I for one am not inclined to interfere." Through so-called "code speak" we hear "we know they want these things, but in order to 'stay in business' we won't object." We have already touched on Daniel Berrigan's "conniving silence."

Historically, the Catholic Church has in fact stepped forward to renounce the evils of nationalism, but only in extreme cases. It fell upon the papacy of Pius XI to address the dangers of extreme nationalism, or what I have chosen to call "flag worship." During the 1930's, in his encyclical "Non Abbiamo Bisogno" he defined fascism as an ideology:

> . . .which clearly resolves itself into a true, real pagan worship of the state-a statolatry . . .in contradiction to the supernatural rights of the church.

Regarding the Nazi movement in Germany during that period, we quote another one of Pius XI's encyclicals in 1937, named "Mit Brennende Sorge." The encyclical is quoted as having regarded Nazism as being "a seduction": and then teaches us:

> None but superficial minds could stumble into concepts of a national God, of a national religion; or attempt to look within the frontiers of a single people, within the narrow limits of a single race, God, the Creator of the universe, King and legislator of all nations.

I for one am learning to look at any expression of nationalism with suspicion. I feel a "we versus them" in every expression of nationalism. Most importantly, I fear that most of what we reck-lessly call "patriotism" is actually nationalism in its limited and seemingly harmless forms. But is it "harmless" even in its limited forms? We read earlier about the difference between "patriotism" and "nationalism" by consulting our dictionary. We even dared to see through the façade of nationalism and took a careful look at the military industrial complex. We ended that paragraph by learning that, in the context of the military industrial complex, Dwight D.

Eisenhower's prophetic voice has gone unheeded. We stated that the ". . .military industrial complex saw us coming."

Now we have delved further into nationalism by addressing the potential for idolatry, consistent with Pope Pius XI. If one wishes to use a less annoying or threatening term, we can call it "flag worship." But when one contemplates the horrific amount of money that changes hands when the United States decides to "go to war," BUT ON A PERMANENT BASIS, the real lesson should come home more closely to the comfortable, suburban parish. Not only are resources drained away from the poor through "flag worship," BUT THE ESSENCE OF IDOLATRY IS THAT THE WORSHIPER IS BEING PLAYED BY THE IDOL. SATAN LOVES A WAR, ESPECIALLY WHEN A RICH AND POWERFUL NATION DECIDES TO MAKE IT AN ADDICTIVE BUSINESS ENTERPRISE.

In addition, there appears to be another "Catholic style" to the error of nationalism. It lies not only in the subtle avoidance of the topic by our priests. It lies in another uniquely Catholic manner in which we attempt to define our so-called nation as being "holy" through attempting to align it with expressions of holiness; by attempting to infuse holiness into our "nation". That is, it might even be the case that one "Catholic style" in which this error is made is made through a distorted kind of Marian devotion.

I read Fr. Dorian Llywelyn, S.J.'s book entitled "Toward A Catholic Theology of Nationality" with Chapter Five entitled "Our Lady of All Nations." I should first point out that, up until the time of this writing, I understood Fr. Llywelyn to mean that, at best, the nation state was a tentative institution, or perhaps an "Imagined Community" such as that of Benedict Anderson. But when I read Chapter Five of Fr. Llywelyn's book, I was no longer sure I understood him. In fact, I thought I read him to contradict himself. That is because Fr. Llywelyn, while writing a ". . .Theology of Nationality", on page 225, and he seems to have done so by means of Marianism, or the reverence given to The Blessed Mother, the mother of Jesus. Fr. Llywelyn writes:

It may not at first glance appear to be a sensible idea, let alone a likely one to claim that there are correlations between Marian dogma and devotion and questions of nationality. Indeed, the connections are not always immediately evident. Nevertheless, reflection on these phenomena shows that there are several important connections between them. Not the least of these is the fact that over the last two thousand years, many different ethnic and national communities have adopted the figure of the Virgin Mary as their patroness.[1]

My reply to this observation would be "what does that prove?" Even if I were to somehow review all of the historical instances in which ". . .different ethnic and national communities adopted the figure of the Virgin Mary as their patroness. . ." I wonder how many of those "adoptions" would have occurred on the way to a battlefield while armed to the teeth or during a legislative abandonment of the poor. More importantly, would the Blessed Mother have reciprocated in those "adoptions?" Fr. Dorian appears to suspect that the Blessed Mother's adoption of the various ethnic wars and legislative greed would be automatic.

As to Fr. Dorian's suggestion (and I am assuming I understand him) if and when people may bring their national concerns to the Blessed Mother, she might not automatically bring her patronage to them, and there is good reason to doubt it. That is because if my "nation-ness" consists of a military-industrial complex which maintains an uncounted number of nuclear weapons, (more than we could live to use) and if my "nation-ness" consists of an economic system in which countless people starve and even basic health care is withheld from them because health care remains a privilege as opposed to a right, if my "nation-ness" consists of parishes which maintain a virulent contempt for peacemakers even within Her Son's church, (to include a morbid fearfulness of them on the part of their pastors) I think it very likely that my nation's invoking the patronage and protection of the Blessed Virgin for its sanctity and protection will only bring about some

---

1. Llywelyn, *Toward a Catholic Theology of Nationalism*, 225

pseudo-religious, romantic fantasy on the part of my "nation" (or parish), not to mention justifying their remaining in the business of perpetual warfare.

To date, all of the respected Marian apparitions that any sound mind takes seriously have been granted to humble, innocent, and most importantly, NONVIOLENT people. I never heard of, nor can I envision, Boeing, General Electric, Northrop Grumman, and the pentagon kneeling at Fatima, Lourdes, Guadalupe, or Medjugorje, nor do I expect it to happen. Fr. Llywelyn's implied "reciprocal holiness" probably will not work.

9

Imposing a Remedy

I PROMISED MYSELF I would keep this a "simple little book." I have tried to draw a contrast between authentic holiness and the façade of a "holy country." I hope to share with the reader some helpful thoughts about authentic holiness as opposed to the contrived holiness of the nation-state, mainly because of the horrific suffering that flows from what I have irreverently called "flag worship."

These few paragraphs are a way of attempting to draw the contrast between authentic holiness and "flag worship" by urging that the authentic holiness of each one of us is sought by seeking out the authentic identity within each person as opposed to the highly superficial identity offered by the nation state. I see the Catholic flag-waving zealots of nationalism as being nothing less than purveyors of "spiritual snake oil."

The concept of a Christian woman or man prayerfully attempting to find their "true selves" is to be profoundly contrasted with nationalism. My own experience has been that Thomas Merton, Benedict Groeschel, and Richard Rohr have been among the deepest thinkers and writers on this topic in my lifetime. The issue of our identity both as a spiritual community and as individuals is, I think, essential to overcoming the scourge of nationalism. For that reason, I will try to end with the topic of our "authentic identities" as God's children alone.

Every "competent" spiritual director knows that the ultimate "life task" before every Christian woman or man is to plumb the depths of herself or himself and discover who they really are. Many competent spiritual directors speak of a person's "essence," or the deepest expression of the self: an ultimate identity that is much deeper and much more meaningful than any identity that this world could assign to any one of us.

Most of us never even seek to find ourselves, although many of us think that we already have. We simply live with whatever definition of ourselves we think we can glean from our mortal existence. In the distant past I used to hear "butcher, baker, and candlestick maker." It was a simple poetic way of expressing human identities rooted in trades or secular vocations. But from time to time, we are called to sit quietly in a small still space, to close our eyes to this world and literally beg God for the grace to calmly drift downward and inward to try to meet the yet unseen face that is our "TRUE SELF."

This is not meditation for meditation's sake. This is not proposed as a remedy for mere vocational dilemmas, pseudo enlightenment, or even some expression of health-seeking. This is a demanding, yet crucial in-depth search for the only self that God really knows and the only self that God has created.

Think of all of the personal historical "accidents" that make up our lives. Our parents and the names and the lives that they "assigned" to us. The homes in which we were raised. The places to which we traveled. Think of our marriages, our children, and the groups of people to which we belong. Then notice that when one of us meets another person for the first time, we promptly "introduce" ourselves in order to define ourselves for the benefit of the other person. But this is rarely, if ever, who we really are. This is a superficial definition of our mortal travels through a world that is destined to discard us into eternity. Only those of us who painstakingly undertake the journey to our true selves, our "essence," can even hope to even approach knowing who we really are.

Now, take the woman or the man who has braved this journey and try to introduce her or him to the world of nationalism. She or he will know that identifying with a nation state is an utterly pointless and wasteful, even blasphemous exercise. They know that they are God's children and that no other definition will suffice.

The "essence" of who we are is juxtaposed against our purported national identity through which we would find ourselves literally killing or supporting that killing to be "someone we cannot be."

I promised myself this would be a "simple little book", and this is as good a place as any to end it. As explained, I began by attempting to write a reply to an article in the June 2017 edition of Commonweal by Dr. Schlabach about the so-called "Just War Theory." After answering the article, I was unable to stop writing for the simple reason that, apparently, the issue of the "Just War Theory" cannot be discussed alone. Too many other issues or problems necessarily flow from it. I hope I succeeded in addressing what I took to be the ultimate issues that accompany the problem; namely nationalism and its inherent idolatry. The "false religion" of nationalism is herein juxtaposed against the authentic version of the Catholic Christian faith. If the reader gave himself or herself a chance, the folly of nationalism will have come to the surface.

God willing, both we and our parishes will grow into that realization. I realize that it is annoying to have one's world view challenged. The ultimate expression of this hope is that the "essence" of who we really are will, after prayerful consideration, surface and we will no longer find ourselves supporting suffering and killing in an effort to become someone we should never be.

Bibliography

Anderson, Benedict. *Imagined Communities*. London: Verso, 1992

Berrigan, Daniel. *Isaiah*. Minneapolis: Augsburg Fortress, 1996

Conference of American Catholic Bishops, 1983

D. Dunning and J. Kruger, *Journal of Personality and Social Psychology*, Vol. 82 (2002) 189–92

Eisenhower, Dwight, Farewell Speech to The American People, 1961

Hillis, Gregory. "Thomas Merton Can Still Teach Us A Lot About Nuclear War." America Magazine (April 2022). https://www.americamagazine.org/faith/2022/04/08/russia-ukraine-nuclear-merton-242661

Llywelyn, Dorian, *Towards a Catholic Theology of Nationalism*, Lanham, Md: Lexington, 2010

Metaxas, Eric, *Boenhoffer: Pastor, Martyr, Prophet, Spy*, Nashville: Thomas Nelson, 2003

Ofenboch, Bill Quotation from Mark Coleville Sentencing, Kings Bay Plowshares Seven 2003 Jan. 13, 2020.

Ofenboch, Bill Quotation from Martha Hennessey Sentencing, Kings Bay Plow Shares Seven, Jan. 13 2003.

Romero, Oscar, *Scandal of Redemption*, Plough, 2018

Scheer, Robert, *The Pornography of Power*, New York: Hachette, 2008

Teilhard De Chardin, Pierre. *Divine Milieu*, New York: Harper & Row, 2001

Walzer, Michael, *Just and Unjust Wars*, New York: Basic Books, 1977

Watts, Craig M. "Daring To Call It Idolatry: Nationalism in Worship." Red Letter Christians Magazine (January 2013). https://www.redletterchristians.org/daring-to-call-it-idolatry-nationalism-in-worship